Money Matters and Financial Power of Attorney

A Compassionate and Practical Guide to Fiduciary Responsibility, Aging Planning, and Harmony

Stephanie Goodman

ISBN:
979-8-9954380-9-0 - Paperback

Golden Agreements Publishing

About the Author

Stephanie Goodman is the founder of Golden Agreements, a structured family planning framework that helps families navigate modern aging with clarity, alignment, and intention.

For more than two decades, she has personally navigated the complexities of aging alongside her own parents while guiding others through the responsibilities of Financial and Healthcare Power of Attorney, as well as roles including Trustee, Executor, and Personal Representative. In this capacity, she has faced firsthand the weight of making critical financial, medical, and legal decisions on behalf of those she loves.

Through her own experience, as well as the stories and assistance provided to others, she identified the gap in thoughtful preparation and communication. Her work is rooted in transforming the aging journey from reactive crisis management into intentional family leadership. By helping families define shared values, priorities, and expectations in advance, she equips them to move through even the most difficult moments with clarity, compassion, and confidence.

The Golden Agreements Framework

Focusing on a single issue can seem like the easiest path, but often it's like arguing over one turn in a road trip without ever looking at the map. The real clarity comes when everyone understands the destination. Golden Agreements are built on six pillars:

1. Open Communication
2. Health, Safety and Comfort
3. Organization and Alignment of Legal Documentation
4. Compassionate Vigilance
5. Family Harmony
6. Cost & Time Protection

Each chapter in this guide aligns to one or more pillars to help you move from understanding to action. Difficult conversations often require a "reason" to have them. Consider this list to determine which conversations should be had and why. Visit www.GoldenAgreements.com for articles, products, inspirations and more.

Every chapter also starts with an actual story in italics that exemplifies the reasons these conversations are so important and illuminates how preparation aligns with the foundation of the framework. Every chapter ends with summary "Golden Agreements" of high-level best practices. Some of the stories are from Golden Agreement interactions, some happened to friends which inspired Golden Agreements. Of course, all names have been changed.

Table of Contents

Introduction

Talking about growing older and aging is one of the most difficult talks a family or loved ones can have because it is a direct acknowledgement of a relentless natural cycle. It is the moment we finally stop pretending the world isn't shifting from the comfort of our past and start facing a loss we have spent most of our lives trying to outrun.

Designation as the agent of a loved one through the Financial Power of Attorney is a profound demonstration of love, trust, and confidence in your ability to manage important matters. While many of the items discussed may never need to be acted upon, being prepared to help manage someone's finances carries significant responsibility and requires intentional, thoughtful support. This book is written for the audience of those designated with the authority, but it is useful for anyone planning to assign the authority or those who do not get the legal documents but wish to assist.

Many of the support roles do not require financial power of attorney, but there are preparations that can avert crisis later. Remember that you don't have to shoulder everything on your own. Many tasks can be delegated to family members, friends, or trusted professionals, allowing you to focus on what truly matters. Even if you're stepping into this position without prior experience or preparation, you can approach the journey with compassion and confidence.

This guide is designed to help you prioritize key decisions and illuminate the path forward, providing clarity and support throughout the process. This "handbook" will give you an overview to the actions you can take to make the transition easier and less stressful.

If you're just beginning this journey or already knee-deep in decisions and paperwork, this book offers real-world advice, step-by-step suggestions, and most importantly, a guide to helping your loved one and/or creating better communication for your own journey.

This guide does not offer or substitute legal or medical advice; please consult your professional advisors for legal and medical questions and documents.

Preface

As people live longer and remain independent well into advanced age, aging has taken on a new shape. This independence is a gift and has also ushered families into uncharted territory, where complex medical and financial decisions must often be made without a common understanding or guiding framework. The days of multigenerational living the way aging was done for generations, is nearly a thing of the past.

Golden Agreements was created to meet this moment to help build more informed connections for a new future. Thoughtful preparation helps families move away from crisis-driven decision making by establishing clear values, priorities, and expectations while loved ones are still able to communicate their wishes. When difficult decisions arise, families rely on conversations and documented guidance providing assurance, preserving dignity, protecting resources, and strengthening relationships.

The support roles are often described as acts of trust and love, and they are. What is less often discussed is how complicated and emotionally demanding they can become when families have not clearly communicated their wishes ahead of time.

My own experiences showed me how difficult things become when families don't discuss important priorities and wishes. With my parents, unspoken values created personal struggles that took a deep toll emotionally and financially. My father's fight with ALS and diminished capacity and my mother's desire to be kept alive at all costs (her words after she became ill) caused family tension, poor choices, countless hours of stress, and very high legal fees. Given the extraordinary time and learning I put into my own family, I became a trusted source to others. While my situation was unique to my family, it echoes the lack of communication many families face. There is a difficult line to walk when honoring and balancing someone's wishes and wishing they had made different choices. The devastating stories from other people resonate that we need a better way.

These experiences solidified the powerful truth for me that proactive planning is not just beneficial, it is critical. It is the calm during chaos, the foundation for peace of mind, and the cornerstone of care for the ones we love. This book offers you a head start, to illuminate the path ahead, and to help you avoid many of the common pitfalls.

This book is for everyone who wants to see the aging journey as a collaborative, supportive process. My hope is that by reading this guide you will feel empowered for the aging journey, not overwhelmed. This is the book I wish I had when to navigate the aging journey. While every situation is unique and not every detail in this guidebook will perfectly match your circumstances, the intention is to provide a guidebook of support. My journey led to the creation of Golden Agreements, a solution designed to address these very challenges by offering structured written and video plans that make the process easier for families.

I wish you and your loved ones a peaceful aging journey and hope this guide will be a comforting companion, offering clarity, practical advice, and the reassurance that you are not alone in navigating this deeply personal and important chapter.

CHAPTER 1

Open Communication

The aging journey often takes many unexpected turns. My client, Alice, called distraught that her mother, Margaret, was going to "accidentally kill herself" because her mother insisted on caregiving to her husband who was bedridden in an upstairs room. It involved multiple trips up and down stairs daily and difficult caretaking which created physical wear and safety issues. Margaret rarely left the house, afraid of leaving her husband alone. Alice was beside herself and nervous every time the phone rang from a family member. She knew this was not how her parents intended Margaret to live her life, but the situation seemed like a hopeless sacrifice. This is a common theme: a family that feels that they have no choices.

It doesn't have to be that way. After a long, authentic conversation, it became clear that the barrier to moving out of the two-story home to a place that could offer support was the lack of open communication between her parents. Margaret never complained, she just wanted to "be a good wife." As soon as we discussed the concern with Alice's father, and he understood what was happening, he came to appreciate the earlier agreements the family had made. His concern for his family and their well-being changed his perspective about moving. He didn't want Margaret to be at risk in the way he had not considered, and he wanted her to have more time in her life for other things. Once the entire family understood the stakes, the decision was made to move to assisted living and all the kids helped make the move easier. The family reports everyone's mental and physical health has improved greatly, including her father's recovery progress, since the move.

Building a foundation of understanding, respect, and clear information is the key to a smoother aging journey. Think of it as organizing the toolbox before the work begins. By asking the right questions now, you equip yourself with the necessary tools for the future. Even if your loved one is completely capable of managing their lives right now, having these conversations and organizing documents in advance will save enormous stress, time and money later. An early conversation would have likely led to earlier, better decisions by Alice's parents.

These early conversations help you understand your loved one's values, goals, and insights into their choices. While these dialogues can be uncomfortable, they are also an act of love. Let them know that you are not trying to take over; rather you are trying to champion and support the life they want to lead independently.

Start Early

- o **Be Proactive:** Begin conversations about financial matters and future wishes early, even if your loved one is currently capable of managing without assistance
- o **Prioritize Autonomy:** The goal is to support their wishes and protect their legacy, not to strip them of control
- o **Choose The Right Environment:** Have these conversations in a relaxed, private setting and avoid rushing the process

o   **Establish a Baseline:** Early conversations allow assessment of cognitive capacity and if noted, provide a baseline for monitoring changes

Checklist/Action Steps

- ☐ **Pick a relaxed setting:** Create low pressure environments for the conversations (e.g., walk, coffee, after dinner)
- ☐ **Choose words wisely and listen:** Use language that emphasizes support for their wishes, focusing on their priorities and values so you learn and understand their decision-making process
- ☐ **Map the basics:** Discuss where they bank and how they pay bills
- ☐ **Use a structured guide:** Download the worksheet at www.GoldenAgreements.com to identify the priorities and routines for when assistance is needed
- ☐ **Identify their trusted professionals:** Create a list of their "inner circle" of attorney, CPA, doctors, insurance broker, etc.
- ☐ **Discuss the "Big Four":** Talk about concerns regarding aging, healthcare, housing, and money
- ☐ **Verify legal documents:** Confirm if they have a will, trust, or existing power of attorney documents
- ☐ **Leverage expert resources:** Utilize resources such as "Five Wishes", "Conversation Project", or articles on GoldenAgreements.com
- ☐ **Centralize information:** Use a secure note-taking app or binder to organize notes

The Art of Conversations

Conversations about aging can be delicate, but they are most successful when rooted in respect, curiosity, and shared purpose. Begin by expressing genuine care rather than concern. Framing discussions around mutual goals like maintaining independence, safety, or peace of mind instead of focusing on decline or loss is more effective than focusing on potential decline or loss.

Asking open-ended questions invites dialogue:

- "What matters most to you as you get older? Listen without interrupting or correcting.
- "If I begin to get concerned, what can I do to help you? Small, compassionate conversations often build more trust than a single "big talk."
- "Who do you trust to help you if you begin to struggle with aging issues? Avoid speaking from fear or urgency and instead invite collaboration.

When aging is discussed as a natural stage of empowerment and preparation, rather than a problem to be solved, defensiveness and embarrassment give way to dignity and connection. Use phrases like "I want to make sure we honor your wishes" rather than "You need to start planning."

The hardest part is getting started. These conversations are usually initiated by the one who wants something to change, and change is hard. Try to put yourself in their mindset and approach with compassion.

Golden Agreement Best Practices

- Begin conversations about financial matters and future wishes early, even if your loved one is currently capable of managing independently
- The goal is to support their wishes, not to take over
- Invite others into the conversation, like a spouse or friend, if it makes it easier
- Never assume you know why someone has made the choices they are living with (think of Margaret in the example); ask the questions
- Spread the conversations out over time to both reflect and to avoid overwhelm
- Have these conversations in a relaxed setting and avoid rushing
- Use voice memos or video to record conversations for later review.

CHAPTER 2

Gather and Organize Key Documents

There is no substitute for preparation before a crisis. Bob was at work when he got the call. His mom was in an ambulance on the way to the hospital after a presumed stroke. She was visiting from out of town and was at the market with Bob's daughter when she collapsed unconscious with a seizure. His mom was heading to a hospital that did not have her records, and he was unsure of her primary physician's name, medicine list, or insurance information.

The next few weeks became even more difficult as his mom was unable to communicate any important information. Bob was sure she had done estate planning with an attorney, but he didn't know who to call to get a copy of it and the original was only in paper form at her home far away. He wasn't sure if he had power of attorney for health or financial decisions. He had no idea what her health insurance would cover or who would be financially responsible for the hospital bill. At the same moment he was emotionally overwhelmed by her health challenges, he also had to become strategic about finding a lot of information, from many different sources, very quickly.

You don't want to be frantically hunting for previously available information (like the name of the estate attorney or insurance policy numbers) in a crisis. Creating a central record now will save everyone a lot of stress later. These documents will become more important in time, so building a relationship with the professionals or institutions early and getting your name on file as an authorized contact will make things easier later. The person you are doing this for will need to give written or verbal authorization to have you added to accounts.

What Information to Collect (with permission)

- [ ] **Bank statements, retirement/investment account info**
- [ ] **Insurance policies** (health, life, property, long-term care)
- [ ] **Social Security** number and statement
- [ ] **Mortgage or lease agreements**
- [ ] **Utility bills**
- [ ] **Names and contact information** regarding Wills or Estate document advisors
- [ ] **Credit card, payments schedules** and other regular bill information
- [ ] **ID cards** (driver's license, passport, Medicare, military)
- [ ] **Digital Access Information** (usernames, online accounts, passwords, etc.)
- [ ] **Medication List** and where the medication is ordered from

Where to Keep the Information

- o Fireproof safe at home (labelled clearly)
- o A digital vault
- o Share a summary list (not full documents) with one other trusted person

Who to Call if Information is Missing

- The bank or credit union's customer service
- HR department of their former employer (for pensions)
- Social Security Administration (for Social Security records)
- Medicare or Insurance company
- County recorder's office (for property deeds)
- Financial Advisor
- Estate Attorney

Documents and More: Shadow Tasks

Ask questions and keep a list of "Shadow Tasks", those hidden financial chores a loved one does that no one notices until they stop doing them. This includes things like renewing car registrations, managing yard service payments, or how they handle annual property tax assessments. Documenting these now prevents critical items from falling through the cracks later.

- **Transparency is Key:** Keep your loved one involved in the process to maintain trust.
- **Start with One Category:** If the list feels overwhelming, start by gathering just the primary bank and utility information.
- **Respect Privacy:** Only collect what is necessary and keep all physical and digital copies stored in high-security locations so they know where to find them in an emergency

Golden Agreement Best Practices

- Creating a central record of key documents now saves stress during a crisis; keep a contact list and key documents on your phone for an emergency
- Building relationships with professionals and institutions early will make things easier later
- You will need written or verbal authorization from your loved one to be added as a contact to their accounts. Often these documents include Financial Power of Attorney, but many will accept verbal consent and signatures on in-house documents
- It is never too soon to start collecting information related to "Shadow Tasks"

CHAPTER 3

Legal and Financial Planning and Avoiding Probate

Sometimes you don't know what you don't know. Janet had been helping care for her mother, Carol, for nearly five years. She managed doctor appointments, coordinated home care, and handled many of the daily decisions that allowed Carol to remain comfortably in her home. Janet reached out to Golden Agreements believing that we were only going to be talking about emotional support issues.

Like many families, Janet assumed the important legal and financial plans had already been handled. Her mother regularly said she had "taken care of everything" years earlier with an attorney. Even though Janet was named as the agent with Financial Power of Attorney, she did not ask to see the documents fearing being intrusive. Once we discussed some of the specifics, Janet quickly learned the reality was far more complicated.

Some accounts were titled in a trust while others were not. A small brokerage account and Carol's IRA had no beneficiary designation at all. One property deed had never been transferred into the trust. Because several assets were not properly titled, part of the estate would have had to go through probate. Additionally, Carol had named people who were now deceased in her document. Without proper attention prior to Carol's death, Janet would have experienced an otherwise simple process being stretched into months of legal filings, court supervision, and additional expenses. That was never Carol's intention. She thought everything was covered.

A simple family conversation, and a review of the existing plans with the professionals who created them, prevented the confusion, cost, and family discord.

Designating a Financial Power of Attorney (FPOA) should be a collaborative process; one rooted in transparency, mutual respect, and long-term harmony for everyone involved. All too often, well intentioned people will designate the Power of Attorney, but the person named is never informed or given the document necessary if use is required.

Often, information "holes" exist between professionals as well with the family or loved ones. There may be existing documents held by an attorney, doctors, financial advisors and other professionals that should be analyzed to prevent duplication, oversights, or conflicting information. While it's natural for loved ones to feel hesitant about sharing personal financial or legal information, especially due to privacy concerns or fear of family tension, these conversations are far better had now than amid a crisis. In some cases, involving the professionals who created the documents, such as attorneys or financial planners, can ease the discussion and provide clarity. The truth is, you can face the discomfort now, or face confusion and potential conflict later. While it is not always possible, it is good practices to include all family members to avoid conflict or litigation later.

Checklist

- ☐ **Review their will** to make sure it updated. Where is the original?
- ☐ **Check trust documents** and understand the terms during their lifetime; especially if a revocable living trust exists
- ☐ **Call/go online with the insurance company** to confirm beneficiaries are current
- ☐ **Check the asset titles and provisions for assets.** To avoid probate, make sure assets are included in the Trust or other legal instruments
- ☐ **Set up a meeting** with the financial advisor, bank, or any other institution in charge of the money
- ☐ **Look at retirement accounts** (IRA, 401k) to confirm consistency and current wishes for named beneficiaries (sometimes the people named have already passed)

Avoiding Probate: Understanding the importance

According to the American Bar Association, approximately 55% of Americans die without a will or estate plan, meaning the distribution of their assets is left to probate courts and intestacy laws (the legal state of dying without a will). In essence, the assets of the loved one are still "owned" by them after they pass, and their heirs need a judge to grant permission for them to be transferred.

Probate is a slow, public, and often expensive legal process that ties up a loved one's assets after death if proper documents have not been prepared in advance. Probate can take months, often years, during which time family members or loved ones may not be able to access needed funds or gain title to property. Worse, it invites conflict when there's ambiguity or disagreement about what the deceased person intended. Probate also becomes a matter of public record, meaning anyone can access details about the estate, beneficiaries, and financial holdings. For families who value privacy, simplicity, and timely resolution, avoiding probate is a critical part of end-of-life planning.

Strategic Measures to Bypass Probate

To steer clear of probate, individuals need to establish certain legal tools in advance. The most common is a revocable living trust, which allows assets to pass directly to heirs without going through a court-approved process. Assets titled in the name of the trust (such as homes, bank accounts, or investments) are distributed according to the trust terms and outside the probate system. Other tools include beneficiary designations (on life insurance, retirement accounts, etc.), payable-on-death (POD) or transfer-on-death (TOD) accounts, and joint ownership with right of survivorship. Each of these strategies needs to be used carefully and consistently to be effective.

Beyond a trust, ensure every financial account has a Payable on Death (POD) or Transfer on Death (TOD) designation. These simple designations allow funds to bypass probate and move immediately to the beneficiary, providing vital liquidity for funeral costs and immediate expenses. Always confirm that these designations match the instructions in the Will or Trust to prevent legal conflict.

There are many options for getting these documents. The most important part is knowing if every step has been completed to make sure it is legal and valid. As Financial Power of Attorney, or the one helping with oversight, you can make sure your loved one is prepared. For more information, it is best and easiest for families should consult with an estate planning attorney in their state, as laws vary. Free and trustworthy resources include: Nolo's Estate Planning Center, AARP's Probate and Estate Basics, and local county probate court websites often explain processes and provide forms. Many states offer free legal aid clinics or online guides through their state bar associations. A proactive conversation now can spare your family stress, cost, and heartache later. While online forms are easy to access, a more thorough analysis and complex situations will require a qualified attorney to help explain your options. Be sure to look at the documents, if for no other reason, there may be language regarding the Power of Attorney, when it begins (immediate versus springing) and specific durable powers.

Use the opportunity to make sure their assets have been protected from going through probate. This information is for general use only. Please consult an attorney or professional regarding probate for your individual circumstance.

Compassion Through Understanding

Talking to your loved ones about the plans they've made, whether it's a will, trust, insurance policy, or any other legal document, isn't just about paperwork; it's about honoring the deeply personal choices they've made for their life and legacy. These documents often reflect values, fears, hopes, and priorities that may have never been openly discussed. Even casually asking where things are stored can feel intrusive if not approached with care. It's important to remember that for many people, sharing this kind of information means making private decisions public sometimes for the first time. Approach these conversations with sensitivity and respect, recognizing that your intention is not to take over, but to support their wishes and protect what matters to them most. Take the time to ask questions early, when thoughtful answers from your loved one can guide later choices on their behalf.

Golden Agreement Best Practices

- Understanding existing plans prevents duplication and conflicting efforts: ask their attorney or professional for a "review meeting" to confirm that everything aligns and bring copies of signed related documents from all professionals involved (for example, bring the Advance Healthcare Directive which may have been signed and on file with a doctor)
- Facing discomfort now by having these conversations avoids confusion and conflict later
- Avoiding probate is crucial for privacy, simplicity, and timely resolution of an estate
- Provide proper documentation to the legal and health professionals before there is a crisis

CHAPTER 4

A Trusted Advocate with Financial Power of Attorney

The best tool for making ethical decisions throughout the aging journey is to understand and honor the wishes of your loved one. When David's father, Allen, gave him Financial Power of Attorney, David assumed the role would mostly involve helping with bills and paperwork if his father ever needed assistance.

Years later, as Allen's health declined, David began reviewing the financial plans his father had put in place. While doing so, he discovered that much of the estate had been structured in ways that didn't feel entirely fair to all the children and grandchildren.

David found himself wrestling with a difficult thought: if he had the authority over the finances, should he quietly "adjust" a few things to make the outcome feel more balanced or advocate for a full estate rewrite?

When David brought the situation to a Golden Agreements conversation, and the family was included in the conversation, the discussion shifted his perspective. The role of Financial Power of

Attorney was not to reinterpret his father's decisions or reshape the estate according to what seemed fair to him at the time. His father had the capacity to contemplate his decisions earlier and had codified his intentions. His fiduciary duty was to faithfully carry out his father's wishes and protect the plans his father had intentionally created even if he didn't entirely agree with them.

By openly discussing the responsibilities of the role and the boundaries of the authority granted under the Power of Attorney, David gained clarity about the job he had accepted: not to change the plan, but to advocate for the person who created it.

Taking on the role is far more than just writing checks. It comes with a **fiduciary duty** that means you are legally and ethically required to act in the best interests of the person that you are helping. You cannot make decisions that benefit you personally, and you must always keep their wishes, values, and priorities front and center. This very important job naturally also includes making sure assets are protected from poor decision making, fraud, and keeping your loved one safe from missed bill payments, etc.

Definition of Fiduciary Duty

A fiduciary duty is a high standard of care imposed by law or equity. A fiduciary is required to demonstrate unwavering loyalty to the principal, to whom they owe their duty. They must prioritize the principal's interests above their own and refrain from deriving personal profit from their fiduciary position (Cornell Law School).

- o **Loyalty:** Always act in the other person's best interest.
- o **Care:** Make decisions with thoughtfulness, caution, and due diligence.

o **Transparency**: Keep detailed records and be prepared to explain your choices.

o **Accountability**: You may be held legally responsible if you misuse your authority.

Understand the Power You've Been Granted: Step-by-step

- [ ] **Locate the Power of Attorney (POA) document**
- [ ] **Make sure it is signed, notarized, and legally valid in your state**. Read it carefully, it will specify what financial actions you are allowed to take.
- [ ] **Determine whether your authority is Immediate or Springing:**

  o **Immediate:** Starts immediately and continues if they become incapacitated

  o **Springing:** Only activates when a doctor certifies incapacity

- [ ] **Register or provide the POA with financial institutions**

  o `Most institutions will allow a copy of the POA and valid ID but check requirements

  o Some banks require their own POA form so inquire in advance.

- [ ] **Keep a copy on your phone and a paper copy easily accessible**

What a Financial POA Agent CAN Do (If Authorized)

- o Manage bank and investment accounts
- o Pay bills
- o File taxes
- o Handle real estate and investments
- o Fund a trust (transferring assets into an existing trust, if permitted)
- o Consult with attorneys or advisors to fully understand and help carry out financial responsibilities
- o In some cases, create or update beneficiary designations; but only if the POA specifically grants that power.

What a Financial POA Agent CANNOT Do

- o **Create or revise a Will independently.** Wills must be personally signed by the individual (with capacity) and witnessed in accordance with state laws
- o **Intentionally commingle personal funds.** Maintain entirely separate bank accounts for the person you are helping and keep a "paper trail" of transactions, especially reimbursements.
- o **Amend or revoke a Trust:** Consult an attorney to see if the Trust document explicitly gives that power to an agent acting under POA
- o **Make decisions after the principal's death.** POA authority ends at death
- o **Require Authorization by Third Parties.** Some banks or institutions may refuse to honor an older or unfamiliar POA unless it has been recently executed, state-compliant, or specifically tailored to their requirements
- o **Breach Fiduciary Duty.** The agent must always act in the

best interest of the principal, not themselves or others. Breach of this duty can lead to legal liability or court action

Important Note

This information is generalized and you should consult with a local attorney to understand state specific information. If changes to estate plans are needed, the principal must make them while still mentally competent. If capacity is lost, a court-appointed conservatorship may be needed to seek any changes, though courts are typically reluctant to allow major estate plan alterations. Planning early prevents these challenges.

For Further Reference

American Bar Association; Powers of Attorney FAQ

Consult an elder law attorney or estate planning attorney if you are facing a complex situation involving trust amendments and diminished capacity.

Bank legal or trust department

Golden Agreement Best Practices

- As the FPOA Agent, you have a fiduciary duty, meaning you must legally and ethically act in the best interests of the person you're helping
- You cannot make decisions that personally benefit you
- Consult with the attorney who created the documents giving authority if you have any questions about specific roles and responsibilities
- Each institution may have their own requirements to be met before authorizing Power of Attorney
- Consult with each bank or institution for their requirements
- There may be legal consequences if actions are taken and later challenged by family or others. Agents should notify relevant parties before acting.
- Your authority to use the Financial Power of Attorney ends upon death

CHAPTER 5

The Hidden Financial Risk of Not Giving Up the Car Keys

This situation is very personal for me. I spent years trying to convince my stepfather that his driving was a serious health, safety, and financial risk. As a stepchild, I felt powerless to enforce "taking away the key." His own children, who were not local, declined to get involved. His license was suspended during a renewal test and later reinstated. His intrinsic need to maintain independence led him to risk the physical and safety of others. His denial about how dangerous he was on the road became a financial risk to the very essence of my mother's ability to maintain living at home and aging-in-place. One significant accident could have ruined both financially.

This is where I learned about the options available to families. Ultimately, it was a doctor/hospital that reported to the DMV that he was no longer capable of driving. It was two hard fought years of fear and aggravation. If Golden Agreements had existed earlier, we would have had a family conversation long before it was needed to establish responsibilities, structures, and agreements to keep everyone safe.

As a loved one ages, continuing to drive can become more than just a question of safety; it can quietly open the door to serious or catastrophic financial and health risks. Beyond the obvious concerns of physical harm, there is a ripple effect that can impact everything from insurance rates to legal liability and the protection of lifelong assets. If you have been trusted with Financial Power of Attorney, or oversight of financial matters, part of your role is to help anticipate and prevent these types of exposures. Looking out for their financial wellbeing includes making sure they are not unknowingly putting their independence, resources, or legacy at risk behind the wheel.

Data Confirms Significant Risks Rise with Age

1. According to the National Highway Traffic Safety Administration (NHTSA) data, the proportion of all fatal crashes involving drivers aged 65+ rose from 11% in 2001 to 19% in 2021.
2. Among adults aged 65+, motor vehicle crashes account for 12.5% of unintentional injury deaths.
3. Data from the Insurance Institute for Highway Safety (IIHS) confirm that fatal crash rates per mile traveled increase noticeably starting at age 70-74 and are highest for drivers 85+.

Family Impact

o **Independence vs Freedom:** Driving is often equated with independence so giving up driving is often seen as giving up freedom. This perception explains why the conversation is so hard, and why there is often resistance to both the notion and the conversations. It takes time and patience to see the difference between mobility and independence.

o **Financial Exposure**: Delaying the decision to stop driving can lead to avoidable accidents, significant insurance liability, or even lawsuits that target personal assets.

o **Preserving Dignity**: Your goal is not to take away control; it is to preserve dignity and protect them financially from a single life-altering event.

Warning Signs That Consequential Risk is Growing

Pay attention to these driving behaviors that can lead to health and financially costly incidents. Most people know they are experiencing some issues before they are willing to discuss their concerns. Opening the conversation early helps build trust so that adaptive measures can be taken before the dreaded "taking the keys".

o Minor accidents or "close calls"
o Getting lost on familiar routes
o Confusion at intersections or traffic signals
o Driving too fast, too slow, or erratically
o Vision or hearing decline
o Medication that affects alertness
o Anxiety, fear, or irritability while driving

Real Financial Exposure (even from a single event)

o Insurance exclusions: Some policies will not cover damages if a driver is deemed unfit or driving on an invalid license
o Lawsuits: If your loved one or parent injures someone, their estate, savings, or home could be at risk

o   Medical costs: Injuries from an accident can lead to hospital bills and long-term care needs

o   License suspension: Failing a DMV driving test can result in a permanent revocation, making future planning more crisis initiated

o   Increased insurance premiums

o   Loss of insurance coverage

o   Vehicle damage

o   Injury liability lawsuits

How to Protect Your Loved One (and Their Finances)

Start early and talk openly. Consider these strategies:

o   **Create a "Golden Agreement" about their values and priorities around driving before it is too late**: A written or video-recorded plan made while they are still fully capable of stating what conditions they would like to use to measure to decide when it is time to stop driving. An example would be "If you stop allowing me to drive your children because you feel I'm a danger, that would be reason to look at stopping altogether".

o   **Identify trigger events together**: Agree on what events will indicate it is time to stop driving

o   **Focus first on dangerous conditions**: Be specific to include driving concerns they currently have about driving in bad weather, night driving, or other concerns and use them to start driving assistance programs on a limited scale

o   **Assess the risk**: Enroll your loved one in a driver's refresher course for seniors

- o **Plan ahead**: Help plan the outings for the day for efficiency and less time on the road
- o **Rely on Resources**: Use Golden Agreements articles on Difficult Conversations for more ideas
- o **Foster safety**: Be receptive to concerns about close calls and fears. without overreacting or creating shame

Introduce Alternatives

Not every concern requires fully giving up driving. It is most helpful and a natural progression towards stopping if you have conversations that feel safe for your loved one to admit to limitations as they happen. For example, if you hear "I'm not driving at night as well as I used to," think about your response as building trust, not trying to take over.

- o **Appreciate the observation** *"I'm really glad you told me that. Night driving is definitely harder. What if we just make evenings easier and plan rides when it's dark? That way you still go everywhere you want during the day."*
- o **Frame it as adapting, not losing independence** *"You've always been practical about things that change. Maybe this is just another adjustment like when you switched to automatic bill pay. We could look at a few options, so driving doesn't have to be the only way you get around."*
- o **Emphasize partnership and respect** *"You've made smart decisions your whole life. I trust your judgment. If driving is starting to feel stressful, let's figure out together what would make you feel most comfortable and still keep you doing the things you enjoy."*

When the time comes, start introducing alternatives on days that may be more difficult to drive due to poor weather

o   Ride-sharing apps (Uber, Lyft)
o   Senior shuttle services
o   Family transportation schedules
o   Grocery and medication delivery

Overcoming Strong Resistance

In some cases, safety requires firmer action:

o   Ask their doctor to evaluate or discuss driving readiness
o   Report to the DMV (can be done anonymously without the driver receiving notice) if legal in your state
o   Consult an elder law attorney about guardianship or financial protection
o   As a last resort, disable the vehicle or hold the keys until a safer plan is in place

A Financial Responsibility to Care

If you are the agent of the Financial Power of Attorney (FPOA), protecting your loved one's assets can include addressing driving risks:

o   Check regularly that they remain insurable and covered
o   Prevent lawsuits that could harm their estate
o   Help them maintain independence in safe, alternative ways
o   Involve others to share the burden as well help influence the decision to stop driving
o   Review their insurance coverage and consider adding a liability "Umbrella" for an extra layer of protection

Golden Agreement Best Practices

- Continuing to drive beyond safe capacity can lead to serious financial risks beyond physical harm; age is not the determining factor alone
- Your role as FPOA Agent includes anticipating and preventing these exposures to protect their assets and independence
- The conversation about giving up driving is difficult because it often represents a loss of independence. Compassionate vigilance will lead you and your loved one to stop driving when the time is necessary to do so
- Involve other family members and loved ones if it will help the situation
- Begin offering alternatives and solutions for slow integration before the problem is only resolved by taking the keys

CHAPTER 6

Knowing When to Step In

The act of helping is often misinterpreted as interfering. Anna knew things were changing but honored how independently her mom had always lived her life. Her mom fiercely protected her ability to manage her own finances and would often get a little angry if Anna overstepped any boundaries trying to be helpful. Anna felt afraid of mentioning anything that might be interpreted as questioning capacity rather than opening a dialogue.

On one visit, Anna noticed stacks of mail in the house which was unusual for how her mom conducted her bill paying. When Anna saw a notice for electricity to be turned off due to nonpayment, Anna became alarmed and asked her mom about it. The explanation was that there was an error at the billing level and that she had already paid the bill. Unconvinced and concerned about the CPAP at night, Anna suggested her mother call the utility and confirm that there would be no discontinuation of service. Anna stayed to listen to the conversation. The representative confirmed no payment had been received and shutoff was still scheduled.

At that moment, Anna recognized that it was time to begin better oversight of her mom's bills and general organization. By setting up automatic bill payments and third-party late bill notifications, Anna did not start the process by taking over, she offered oversight. This built trust between Anna and her mother that has been positive and helpful as her mother's capacity has continued to decline.

Even with the most thoughtful preparation, life continues to unfold in unexpected ways. As your loved one gets older, you may notice changes that suggest it is time to be more involved. Recognizing these changes is not about hovering or overreacting; it is about being present, observant, and prepared to respond with care. Remember that these changes, such as forgetfulness, distraction, or simple mistakes, are part of the human experience at any age. They are not intentional acts, but natural signs of aging.

Your role is not to take over; step in with kindness and support your loved one's independence and dignity for as long as possible. Compassionate vigilance is the key...watching not out of fear, but from love and concern.

What to Watch for and How to Respond

The "Baseline" Comparison

When you notice a change, compare it to the "baseline" you observed prior. Is this a sudden drop in ability, or a slow shift? Rapid changes often signal reversible medical issues (like a UTI or medication interaction), while slow shifts may indicate a need for more permanent "co-pilot" support.

- o Recognizing changes is about compassionate vigilance, not hovering or overreacting.
- o Forgetfulness or mistakes are natural signs of aging, not intentional acts; vigilance over these limitations protects your loved one.

- o Your role is to support their independence and dignity for as long as possible. Be mindful of the transition from observer to active assistance and include them as much as possible.
- o Solicit help from friends, neighbors, family, or professionals to provide appropriate levels of support and prevent your own burnout.

Health Clues (Involve Agent with Healthcare Power of Attorney)

- o **Missed medications**? → Call their pharmacy and doctor to discuss simplified packaging or automated reminders.
- o **Missed appointments**? → Call the doctor, reschedule, and ask for future notifications
- o **More ER visits**? → Ask for a care conference with their healthcare team and identify underlying risks
- o **Diagnosis of dementia**? → Monitor decline and start using your POA authority when applicable.

Financial Clues

- o **Bills stacking up**? → Set up auto-pay through their bank or offer to sit together once a week to sort through mail
- o **Scams or strange charges**? → Contact their bank's fraud department immediately
- o **Identity Theft Concerns or Limited Financial Actions Taken**→Consider placing a credit freeze with Equifax, Experian, and TransUnion which does not affect the credit score

Behavioral Clues

- o **Isolating from friends**? → Gently ask how they're feeling and encourage social connection
- o **Minimizing self care routines**? → Create checklists and reminders to maintain daily rhythm
- o **Forgetting familiar names, places, or directions**? → Consult with the designated Healthcare Power of Attorney or the doctor

Response Plans

- o **Check communication channels**: Regularly check physical mail, emails, and voicemail for urgent notices or past due alerts
- o **Audit statements**: Review statements for late fees or odd withdrawals.
- o **Document everything**: Begin logging everything you help with in a simple spreadsheet or notebook to maintain the transparency required of a fiduciary. Find a simple and easy way to do it
- o **Simplify systems**: Increase oversight of bill paying and setting up simplified systems that make it easy for your loved one to stay involved

Golden Agreement Best Practices

- Discuss change when you notice them. Recognition is about compassionate vigilance, not hovering or overreacting
- Forgetfulness or mistakes are natural signs of aging, not intentional acts but a call to assess the need for additional support
- Your role is to maintain their independence and dignity for as long as possible.
- Recognize that ignoring the problems or avoiding hard conversations can have serious consequences, far worse than the stress of early intervention

42

CHAPTER 7

Expanding Support for Changing Needs

Obviously, some slips have no important consequences, but others can be more serious. An expensive, avoidable situation occurred that threatened losing the family home. Jerry was a very independent 86-year-old who had always taken excellent care of himself and his finances. All four of his kids assumed he had managed his money well and that when the end of life came for him, they would have a smooth transition well planned by their father.

It turned out, that there had been an understandable mishap with ongoing automatic payments for Jerry's mortgage. By the time it was uncovered, the family had to hire an attorney as well as pay the longstanding missed payments to avoid an imminent foreclosure. The four kids all had very different opinions on everything from how to look after their father in the future to who should be paying the bills to undo this unfortunate situation. The family disharmony took a significant toll on everyone.

This story is one of so many where delay in expanded support through the aging process leads to an avoidable challenge. A family plan would have eased or prevented this misstep.

One of the hardest parts of watching someone we love age is experiencing the difference between the independence they used to have, and the need for more assistance. Don't take it personally if their preferred level of involvement differs from what you think is necessary. Approach the situation with humility and patience to respect their autonomy while safeguarding their wellbeing. It is a rare person that does not place high value on their independence and dignity, and most people are willing to "fight" for it.

This is the stage where preparation turns into active support. Think of it not as taking control, but as becoming a steady co-pilot; someone who is there to help navigate and not to steer the entire journey. It is essential to recognize that stepping in more actively often means your loved one is experiences a loss of independence, something they may deeply cherish and grieve. Acknowledge that loss with empathy. Let them know you are not here to override their choices, but to uphold their wishes with care and respect. Offer help in ways that preserve their voice, invite their input, present choices rather than directives, and check in often. Try not to take it personally if they are angry about how involved they want you to be if it does not align with the needs you are seeing. You were asked to take on this role when there was greater clarity that this day would eventually come. By showing up with humility and patience, you become not just a co-pilot, but a partner who honors their autonomy while supporting their wellbeing. It is not your job to take the controls and there is no "right way" to do everything. You have been asked to help.

How to Increase Involvement

- o Offer to balance their checkbook or review statements together.
- o Become a cosigner or POA on bank accounts (not just online access through a password which can violate the bank's Terms of Service).
- o Help schedule automatic bill payments.
- o Register your name with loan or mortgage companies for notification if payments are missed
- o Update or verify Social Security, VA, or pension benefits.
- o Call utilities and service providers to protect continuity by adding your contact information to be notified before service termination (the account holder will need to authorize).

Online Tools to Simplify Paying Bills

- o Software like Quicken or YNAB (for budget tracking)
- o Truebill (to find and cancel unused subscriptions)
- o Family access settings through Medicare or MySSA.gov

Golden Agreement Best Practices

- This stage is about active support and becoming a "co-pilot," not taking full control unless necessary
- Acknowledge their potential loss of independence and include them to their capacity
- Uphold their wishes, present choices, and invite their input
- Show up with humility and patience, even if their desired involvement differs from perceived needs
- The tasks of day-to-day life do not have to be serious and burdensome. Plan positive rituals such as having lunch together at a favorite place or doing something fun together after the "business" part of the day is done.

CHAPTER 8

Navigating Cognitive Changes

Switching from a lifetime of caregiving to needing help is one of the most painful parts of aging. It is particularly heartbreaking when a parent seems threatened or angry at the idea of having a child help them. Don was the kind of father that made every decision for himself. He paid every bill on time and made cost conscious choices in his spending.

In our family meeting, his son Kevin shared an illuminating story of finding out that his father had been paying his credit cards in full but had missed that there were several charges in Russian rubles each month. Don was careful with paying the bill but had lost his capacity to identify fraudulent charges in a world where charge names are often complicated.

The family recognized the need for more involvement despite Don's common refrain "It's my money". The solution we arrived at was a monthly lunch at Don's favorite sandwich shop, with Kevin, where Don would share his pile of paid bills and accept help checking to make sure they were accurate. In a follow up email, it was shared that the practice of doing it together ultimately created a trust that Don felt comfortable allowing Kevin to take over the bill paying entirely following a medical event.

It's natural to notice changes in an aging loved one's memory or thinking. Occasional forgetfulness, like misplacing a bill or needing a reminder for a due date, is a normal part of aging and often tied to common issues such as stress, medications, or fatigue. But when confusion, repeated errors, or avoidance of financial discussions begin to surface, these may be early signs of cognitive change. Understanding the difference between "typical forgetfulness" and "warning signs" allows you to step in with both compassion and foresight.

When it comes to financial matters, readiness is protection. Delaying the organization and sharing of important financial details is one of the biggest money risks families can face. If an aging loved one becomes unable to recall account details, passwords, or contact names, recovering that information later can be both overwhelming and time-consuming. Creating a clear, confidential record of key accounts, insurance policies, legal documents, and trusted advisors creates continuity and peace of mind. Early involvement also allows you to observe potential significant red flags such as missed payments, duplicate donations or payments, or unusual spending that may indicate confusion or vulnerability to scams. Being formally listed with professionals and institutions ensures two-way communication if important issues are identified.

Family members play a crucial role in helping maintain financial stability and autonomy. Encouraging open conversations, setting up systems like automatic bill pay, and gradually establishing shared oversight can prevent crisis and preserve dignity. Taking action early, while cognitive capacity is sharp, ensures planning is effective, collaborative, and less stressful for everyone involved.

Normal Aging vs. Early Signs of Disease

For specific symptoms or for diagnosis, always consult a doctor. This chapter is here to inform, support, and help families recognize early signs while preparing to act with care and not suggest a substitute for medical evaluation.

Normal age-related cognitive decline is simply part of getting older. The brain has a natural way of slowing down a little at a time, not always a sign of disease. It might take longer to recall a name, find the right word, or learn something new, but these changes are mild and don't interfere with the ability to live independently or make sound decisions. It is normal to forget your keys if you have the capacity to retrace your steps to find them. Unlike dementia, which involves ongoing and disruptive memory loss, normal cognitive aging reflects a shift in how the brain processes and retrieves information while still preserving wisdom, emotional understanding, and perspective.

Dementia and cognitive impairment go beyond the expected changes of normal aging. They signal a deeper disruption in how the brain manages memory, reasoning, language, and everyday function. When memory loss starts to interfere with independence, like getting lost on familiar routes, forgetting to pay bills, or struggling to follow conversations, it is time to take notice. These changes aren't just "senior moments"; they can indicate conditions such as Alzheimer's disease or other forms of dementia that require medical attention and planning. If you notice ongoing confusion, mood shifts, or withdrawal from social activities, do not ignore them and schedule a medical evaluation with a primary care doctor or neurologist. Early assessment can often uncover reversible causes (like a UTI or medication side effect) and help create a care plan that preserves safety, dignity, and quality of life. Acting early allows families to prepare legally and emotionally, so decisions are made with clarity rather than crisis.

Early Signs That Deserve Attention

- o Frequent memory lapses that disrupt daily life (e.g., forgetting important dates, repeating the same questions, or losing track of conversations)
- o Confusion about time, place, or familiar routes
- o New difficulty managing household tasks, medications, or finances
- o Noticeable changes in judgment, mood, or personality
- o Trouble following conversations or instructions
- o Withdrawing from social activities they once enjoyed

Unlike normal aging, symptoms of dementia are a group of conditions that affect memory, reasoning, and independence. The symptoms progress over time and interfere with everyday living. When these signs appear, it is time to move from casual observation to active support. Discuss your concerns with a doctor.

Risks of Ignoring or Minimizing Cognitive Decline

Families often minimize early symptoms out of love, fear, or the hope that things will improve. There are several trusted resources available for assessing cognitive decline, ranging from self-assessments to professional evaluations. The Alzheimer's Association offers free online tools and guidance for recognizing early warning signs and finding local memory clinics. Primary care physicians can administer brief screening tests such as the Mini-Mental State Examination (MMSE) or Montreal Cognitive Assessment (MoCA) to evaluate memory, reasoning, and attention. For more detailed evaluations, neurologists, neuropsychologists, and geriatric specialists can perform comprehensive cognitive testing to help identify causes, track changes over time, and guide appropriate next steps in care. Unfortunately, ignoring signs can create serious risks.

Health and Safety Risks

- o **Delayed diagnosis** means missed opportunities for early intervention or treatment
- o **Increased vulnerability** to falls, wandering, medication errors, or household accidents
- o **Overlooked causes** such as medication side effects, thyroid issues, or infections

Financial and Legal Risks

- o **Financial exploitation or mismanagement** may occur as judgment declines
- o **Unpaid bills, scams, and errors** can cause lasting financial damage
- o **Lost time for legal planning**, such as Power of Attorney, Advance Directives, or Wills, can leave loved ones unprepared when decision-making is needed most

Emotional and Relationship Risks

- o **Erosion of trust**: Dismissal of concerns can make the person feel unheard or embarrassed
- o **Family conflict**: Differing opinions about what's "really going on" can divide siblings or caregivers

o **Isolation and depression**: Minimizing symptoms can deepen shame and withdrawal

Caregiving and Planning Risks

o **Crisis-driven decisions**: Waiting too long often leads to sudden emergencies such as hospitalizations, unsafe driving, or abrupt care placements

o **Caregiver burnout**: Delayed action can overwhelm families

o **Loss of autonomy**: The person loses the chance to voice their wishes while they still can

Ignoring cognitive decline is not just risky; it prevents families from having calm, compassionate, and dignified conversations that protect everyone's well-being.

Practical Support Regardless of Cause or Diagnosis

When concerns first arise, gentle, steady action makes a world of difference.

o **Start with Observation**: Keep a log of changes in memory, mood, or daily functioning. This helps doctors identify patterns and possible causes

o **Support Daily Tasks**: Offer help with bills, medication organization, grocery lists, or meal prep without taking over

o **Use Reminders and Aids**: Calendars, alarms, and labeled cabinets empower independence and reduce frustration (see memory tools at www.GoldenAgreements.com)

o **Encourage Routine**: Consistent schedules, light exercise, and healthy sleep improve clarity and confidence

o **Stay Connected**: Social engagement through phone calls, visits, group activities boost mood and slows decline

o **Pro tip**: Some studies suggest that green is more recognizable and memorable for older adults who have memory issues when leaving notes or instructions

Talking About Cognitive Concerns

Starting the conversation about memory loss can be delicate. The goal is support, not correction. Facing the signs early does not take away hope, it allows management with a peaceful plan.

o **Use "I" statements**: "I've noticed it's taking a little longer to remember things. Maybe we should check in with the doctor just to be safe."

o **Normalize the experience**: Remind them that changes in memory are common and that getting checked is a proactive, smart choice

o **Invite their perspective**: "Have you noticed any changes that are frustrating or worrying you?"

o **Preserve independence**: "Putting small supports in place can actually help you stay independent longer."

o **Don't try to fix everything in one talk**: Begin small, plant seeds, and return gently over time. The goal is to open the door, not push it open

Conversations Supporting Advanced Cognitive Decline

As dementia or decline progresses, communication requires even more patience and creativity. Support for communicating with someone experiencing advanced cognitive decline or dementia can be found through organizations like the Alzheimer's Association, which offers caregiver training, support groups, and a 24/7 helpline (1-800-272-3900). The Family Caregiver Alliance and the National Institute on Aging also provide free online resources, videos, and communication guides that teach practical strategies for connecting with empathy, reducing frustration, and maintaining dignity throughout the progression of the disease.

- o **Respond to the emotion**, not just the question: If they ask, "When are we going home?", respond to the feeling: "You're safe here with me. It's nice to be somewhere cozy and familiar, isn't it?"
- o **Answer with patience, even if repeated**: Repetition is a symptom, not a choice. Calm, consistent answers are reassuring
- o **Redirect gently**: "That's a good question. While we wait for dinner, would you help me fold these napkins?"
- o **Use visual cues**: A large-print clock, daily schedule, or sign saying "We're home. Dinner is at 6" can provide comfort and reduce repeated questions
- o **Avoid arguing or correcting**: Step into their reality. If they believe it's 1975, talk about that time instead of correcting them

Caregiver Self-Care

Remember that repeated questions are not a test of your patience, they're a call for reassurance. If frustration rises, step away briefly and, if possible, ask another family member to take over. Remind yourself: It's the disease, not the person. Consider adding support to your "village" through support groups, occupational and physical specialists, and planning time for leaving the caregiving environment.

Seeking Professional Guidance

Getting professional input ensures accurate diagnosis and peace of mind. Selecting the right professional, at a manageable cost, for the earliest onset can make the process infinitely easier.

- o Primary Care Physician (PCP): Rules out treatable causes such as thyroid imbalance, vitamin deficiency, or medication side effects.
- o Neurologist or Geriatric Specialist: Provides deeper evaluation, imaging, and memory testing.
- o Neuropsychological Testing: Offers detailed insight into cognitive strengths and weaknesses.
- o Local Resources: The Alzheimer's Association and local Area Agencies on Aging offer education, caregiver support, and planning tools.

Golden Agreement Best Practices

- Recognizing the difference between normal forgetfulness and cognitive decline allows families to act with compassion and foresight preventing confusion, financial errors, and crisis-driven decisions later
- Delaying financial organization increases risks. Establishing a clear record of accounts, passwords, insurance, and advisors ensures continuity and shields loved ones from stress, scams, and lost time during decline
- Early involvement and open communication and shared financial oversight, such as automatic bill pay or joint monitoring, maintain autonomy and trust while safeguarding independence and stability
- Minimizing or ignoring symptoms can lead to health, financial, emotional, and caregiving challenges.
- Approach memory concerns gently with empathy and "I" statements. Seek evaluation from medical professionals, and use available resources like the Alzheimer's Association to plan early and preserve quality of life
- Visit www.GoldenAgreements.com shop for curated and trusted products to assist in the house for memory/cognitive issues

CHAPTER 9

Recognizing and Protecting Against Elder Financial Abuse

A family presented with an unfortunate situation that happens all too common. As Jackie was aging, and requiring extra help around the house, her great-nephew Andrew offered to move in to help. Jackie's two daughters were happy she had a companion and man in the house. It was several months before her duaghters learned that Jackie was buying Andrew food, clothes and gifts. They started to question the motives of Andrew being at the house and felt conflicted in addressing the issue.

Andrew was not on the phone or home during our family conversation and Jackie felt free to talk. It was determined that Jackie didn't feel comfortable with Andrew's requests (which ended up costing more than $15,000) but felt obligated to help her family member. Furthermore, Jackie thought that Andrew's help meant that her daughters would be less burdened.

Jackie and her family fixed the problem, and Andrew was asked to move out. Jackie also added her daughters to her bank accounts so they could watch to make sure she wasn't taken advantage of by anyone else.

Protecting a loved one's legacy is about more than just managing their bills, it can also be safeguarding them from those who would take advantage of their trust or changing cognitive abilities. Elder financial abuse is often called the "invisible crime" because it can happen slowly, behind closed doors, and frequently at the hands of those known best. As a Financial Power of Attorney agent, you serve as the first line of defense in protecting assets. By maintaining compassionate vigilance and setting up structural safeguards, you can ensure your loved one's resources are used for their care and nobody else's gain.

The Reality of Financial Exploitation

Elder financial abuse isn't just limited to "stranger danger" or phone scams. It includes the unauthorized use of funds, property, or assets.

o **The "Trusted" Circle:** Statistically, a significant portion of financial exploitation is committed by family members, caregivers, or "new friends" who gain the confidence of a loved one

o **Cognitive Vulnerability:** Individuals with early-stage dementia or memory loss are at higher risk because they may forget previous transactions or struggle to understand complex financial documents

o **Isolation as a Tool:** Abusers often try to isolate the loved one from other family members to prevent anyone else from seeing the financial records

Red Flags: What to Watch For

- o **Unusual Bank Activity:** Large, unexplained withdrawals, frequent transfers between accounts, or ATM usage by someone who typically doesn't use a debit card
- o **Missing Property:** Items disappearing from the home, such as jewelry, collectibles, or even small electronics
- o **Sudden Legal Changes:** Unexpected changes to a Will, Trust, or Power of Attorney, especially if the senior cannot clearly explain why they made the change
- o **New "Best Friends":** A person who suddenly becomes very involved in offering "financial advice" or asking for "loans"
- o **Unpaid Bills:** Utility shut-off notices or eviction threats despite belief the bills were paid
- o **Password Changes:** Unexplained limited access to wifi, computers, or anything else that suggests someone may have changed passwords

Structural Safeguards: How to Protect Against Abuse

- o **Limit Cash Exposure:** Encourage the use of direct deposit for Social Security or pensions to prevent checks from being stolen from the mail.
- o **Set Up Account Alerts:** Many banks allow a "view-only" access for a secondary contact, or can send text alerts for transactions over a certain dollar amount.
- o **Place a Credit Freeze:** As discussed in previous chapters, freezing credit with Equifax, Experian, and TransUnion prevents new accounts from being opened in their name.
- o **Register with "Trusted Contact" Forms:** Provide your contact information to investment firms and banks as

a "Trusted Contact" so they can call you if they suspect a fraudulent trade or banking activity (permission or Financial Power of Attorney may be required).

o **Conduct Regular Audits:** As a fiduciary, your habit of logging every transaction (as detailed in the Appendix) naturally helps you spot irregularities immediately.

How to Respond if You Suspect Abuse

If you believe exploitation is occurring, do not wait. Early intervention is the only way to recover lost assets and prevent further damage.

1. **Contact the Bank:** Report suspicious activity to the bank's fraud department immediately
2. **Adult Protective Services (APS):** Contact your local APS office. They are trained to investigate financial exploitation while respecting the senior's dignity
3. **Law Enforcement:** If a crime has been committed, such as theft or forgery, file a police report to create a formal paper trail. Don't hesitate to call law enforcement if you suspect physical abuse

Golden Agreements Best Practices

- **Transparency as a Shield:** The best defense against accusations or internal family abuse is radical transparency. By sharing a monthly summary of spending with siblings or other heirs (as discussed in Chapter 9), you create a "community of oversight" that makes it nearly impossible for an abuser to operate in the shadows.
- **Educate Your Loved One:** Gently share information about current scams so they know what to look for without feeling judged.
- **Check the Mail:** Scammers often use "junk mail" sweepstakes to hook seniors into recurring payments.
- **Trust Your Instincts:** If a new person in your loved one's life feels like they are overstepping, they probably are.

CHAPTER 10

Good Practices for Siblings, Family Members, and Other Loved Ones

Everyone knows at least one story where sibling relationships fracture beyond repair during the aging process of a parent. Sandy often said that when the end of her life came, she hoped her children would gather peacefully, share stories, and celebrate the life they had built together.

When a health crisis forced decisions about her care, her children couldn't even think about creating that environment. Years of disagreement about managing Sandy's aging choices had hardened into resentment. One believed she should stay at home no matter the cost or life expectancy. Another believed assisted living was the responsible choice. They had fought for years over the level and type of care she needed.

What Sandy had hoped would be a time of unity became a series of separate conversations, tense phone calls, and decisions made without everyone in the room. The painful reality is that without clear communication and shared expectations ahead of time, the harmony parents hope for can easily unravel when the stakes are highest.

In my experience, families don't fall apart because individuals don't care. They divide with anger because they never aligned on a plan to care together. On some level, every family I've ever worked with has struggled in this arena. There is an art to maximizing peace and harmony while implementing the aging plan. When a loved one begins to age and needs more coordinated support, families and friends enter one of life's most complex seasons. It's a time that tests love, patience, communication, and priorities. Even the most well-intentioned families can find themselves navigating emotional territory unprepared to discuss grief, resentment, guilt, and differing opinions about "what's best." You are not alone.

The key to maintaining peace and connection is not perfection, it is patience, an abundance of communication, and gratitude that there is someone else with whom to share the experience. By establishing clear roles, using kindness as a guiding principle, and treating each other with empathy, families can transform what could be a source of stress into an act of shared love and legacy.

Begin with Shared Intention

Before diving into logistics, families should align around a shared purpose. Pillars of dignity, compassion, and unity are a great place to start. The intentions become the foundation of every conversation and decision. It is not about who is right or more impactful, it is about making the right decisions together.

If you have not already gone through the practice of

establishing Golden Agreements, a family "mission statement" can help. For example:

"We are committed to caring for Mom with respect, clarity, and teamwork. We will communicate honestly, assume good intentions, and act with love."

Revisiting this intention regularly, especially when stress rises, can keep everyone centered.

Distribute Tasks by Strengths and Capacity

Conflict often begins when family members assume unequal or unclear roles. A good plan identifies who will do which tasks so that no one carries the full load alone. Use each person's strengths and availability:

o   The sibling or relative with financial skills can handle bills and budgets.
o   The one nearby can coordinate appointments or check in regularly.
o   The better communicator can update extended family or help manage emotions
o   An out-of-town sibling or loved one can help by managing the digital vault, handling insurance issues, hiring a house cleaner, or assisting with oversight of accounts

These divisions should be flexible and reviewed regularly as needs evolve. It's also wise to rotate high-stress responsibilities (like medical coordination or care scheduling) so no one burns out. Avoid treating one another like co-workers in a transactional role or a job. It is a shared responsibility rooted in care and often given without compensation. It is a team effort and most often no one is being monetarily compensated for their time and energy.

Use a shared document or online tool to track tasks, contacts, and appointments. Transparency eliminates confusion and wards off suspicion and resentment by helping everyone see the full picture.

Lead with Empathy, Not Judgment

Every family member will experience the aging journey and family shifts differently. Some may grieve, some may avoid, others may over-function. Instead of criticizing how someone copes, approach them with curiosity and compassion.

You might say: "I hear something different in your voice this time when talking about mom. How can I help lighten the load?" or "It sounds like you're worried about Dad's decline. What would feel helpful for you right now?"

Empathy softens edges. It reminds everyone that behind each opinion or reaction is love and fear for the same person.

Practice Gratitude Out Loud and Often

Acknowledgment is fuel for harmony. Thanking each other for both big and small contributions builds trust and goodwill. Even if tensions exist, gratitude helps reframe the focus from who is doing it wrong to what is going right.

"Thank you for handling Mom's insurance calls."

"I really appreciate the time you're spending with her. It means a lot."

Some families keep a "gratitude or success text thread" or group message where they share small victories or kind observations about their loved one's progress. It keeps the spirit of appreciation alive amid the logistics.

Communicate Regularly and Clearly

Silence breeds assumptions and assumptions breed conflict.

- o Establish a rhythm of family updates—weekly calls, monthly summaries, or group texts. Choose a communication method that fits everyone's style
- o When families are aligned, decisions are made more efficiently, reducing both emotional strain and unnecessary financial cost

Keep updates factual and emotionally neutral when possible:

- o "Mom's blood pressure medication was adjusted" "The physical therapist said she's improving"
- o "We paid the property tax this week"

When disagreements arise, take a pause before reacting.

- o Revisit the shared intention, listen without interruption, and avoid side conversations that divide siblings into camps
- o If emotions flare, agree to revisit the discussion after 24 hours
- o Calm clarity always leads to better decisions

Respect Boundaries and Individual Lives

- o Not everyone can, or should, be equally involved
- o Circumstances vary: work, distance, finances, and emotional bandwidth. Avoid measuring "love" by hours of care or dollars spent. Recognize that each sibling is contributing in their own way. Some will give time, others

expertise, others financial support

o   Lack of any support by a specific family member may reflect underlying circumstances that deserve understanding rather than added pressure and not leveraged as an additional stress on the process

Instead of resentment, practice understanding:

o   "I know you wish you could be here more often. Your support from afar still matters"

o   Honoring each person's boundary keeps the caregiving environment sustainable for everyone

Use Professionals as Neutral Partners

o   When emotions cloud judgment, neutral third parties can bring perspective. Geriatric care managers, financial advisors, mediators, or elder law attorneys can provide both structure and relief

o   Having an objective guide prevents sibling disagreements from derailing important steps and reinforces the shared goal of your loved one's well-being

o   Golden Agreements offers family consulting for the overall aging process to minimize issues as the challenges become more critical

Keep the Loved One's "Voice" Central

Amid planning and decision-making, it's easy for the aging loved one to fade into the background. This is where the practice of adhering to the principals of Golden Agreements can help. Always return to their wishes, values, and dignity. Ask what matters most to them about autonomy, comfort, home environment, faith, legacy and let those preferences guide action.

"What does peace look like for you, Mom?" "How can we make sure you still feel in control?"

When siblings or loved ones align around honoring the loved one's voice, unity strengthens naturally.

Acknowledge the Emotional Terrain

Caregiving stirs grief before loss, resentment before rest, and fatigue before gratitude. These emotions are normal and naming them can help. There is an abundance of available support for grief.

Encourage each other to rest, seek therapy, or take breaks without guilt. Create a family understanding: "We are all doing the best we can, and it's okay to need time away." Mutual permission to feel and heal preserves compassion across the journey.

Anchor the Process in Love and Legacy

The way siblings navigate this chapter becomes a lasting part of the family story. Years from now, what will you remember: arguments over logistics or the way you pulled together with grace? Love is not measured by agreement but by the willingness to stay connected through difficulty.

What Commonly Breaks Down

Family conflict rarely comes from one major disagreement. It builds from smaller breakdowns and a lifetime of unrelated moments that get applied to the new situation. Lack of clear roles

- o   Poor communication or assumptions
- o   Unequal participation without acknowledgment
- o   Decisions made without transparency
- o   Emotional reactions without space to process

If the problem is disruptive or too challenging, it is strongly recommended to seek professional advice from a therapist, a grief counselor, clergy, or others that everyone will trust.

Golden Agreement Best Practices

- Align early on a shared mission and keep returning to it.
- Divide responsibilities by leveraging individual strengths and a realistic assessment of availability, rather than aiming for equal time allocation
- Communicate openly, kindly, and consistently
- Express gratitude regularly; small acknowledgments go far
- Keep empathy and the loved one's dignity at the center of all decisions

CHAPTER 11

Preparing for End-of-Life & Transitioning

Life after losing a loved one is hard enough, remember there is so much you can do in advance to make things easier for the journey. When Michael's mother Joan began declining, most of the family's focus was on her healthcare. She had always managed her own affairs and often brushed off conversations about paperwork, saying, "My lawyer handled it all."

Michael had been named as Financial Power of Attorney years earlier, and he assumed everything was already organized. During Joan's final months, Michael stepped in to help manage her bills and coordinate with her caregivers without issue.

When Joan passed away, everything changed overnight. The bank account Michael had been using as Power of Attorney was immediately frozen. His authority ended at her death, and the bank required the executor of the estate to take over. Unfortunately, the executor named in Joan's outdated will had passed away years earlier.

As Michael began sorting through paperwork, more issues surfaced. Some accounts had no named beneficiaries and would need to go through probate. Subscription services continued charging her credit card. Thousands of family photos were stored in online accounts no one could access.

Having well-prepared estate documents in place is one of the most thoughtful gifts your loved one can leave behind, regardless of wealth or assets. With the Financial Power of Attorney, you are in a unique position to encourage and help facilitate what happens to all aspects of what they have left behind by planning while your loved one is still able to make decisions confidently. If your loved one has already lost capacity to make those decisions, you still have Financial Power of Attorney and can discuss the necessary arrangements and documents with an attorney or estate planning professional.

A properly executed will and the necessary documents help ensure that their wishes are honored and make the transition after their passing is as smooth as possible for the people they care about. Without these documents, even modest estates can get caught up in probate, a formal court process that can be time-consuming, expensive, and emotionally draining during an already difficult time. By supporting your loved one in creating or updating essential documents, like a will, trust, and named beneficiaries, you help preserve their intentions and protect their legacy. While your legal authority as the Financial Power of Attorney agent may end at the time of death, your continued involvement, guidance, and thoughtfulness can make all the difference. You are not just helping to manage the practical side of things, you are helping to carry forward their life story with care, clarity, and respect.

Preparing for End of Life and Transition

- ☐ Confirm their bills are paid and that services are maintained
- ☐ Make sure there is enough cash available to cover funeral expenses. There may be a delay in accessing additional funds after death
- ☐ Coordinate with caregivers, hospice, and facilities
- ☐ Confirm that estate documents are ready and accessible
- ☐ Gather funeral preferences or decide with a local funeral home
- ☐ Reconfirm that access to bank accounts will be continuous after death with the named executor (estate planning documents need to be to avoid accounts going through probate)
- ☐ Prepare an inventory of "digital hand off" of subscriptions, accounts, digital photos, etc that may require cancellation or distribution

Well-prepared estate documents are a thoughtful gift, that honor a person's wishes and make the transition easier for those they leave behind. As Financial Power of Attorney agent, you can facilitate planning while your loved one still has capacity which minimizes disruption and extra time to the process later.

If capacity is lost, you can still discuss necessary documents with legal professionals. However, some documents cannot be signed by the principal without a court approved conservatorship. To avoid this costly and sometimes difficult step, it is essential that all professionals who are under confidentiality agreements prior to incapacitation have on file documents authorizing conversations with successor Trustees or other designated persons. Ask your lawyers, doctors, financial advisors, and others to provide authorization agreements to be prepared if incapacitation becomes an issue.

Golden Agreement Best Practices

- Proper documents reduce delays, legal costs, confusion, and disagreement, as does avoiding probate.
- Access to documents is critical for easy transition into an estate.
- Loved ones feel more peace knowing that someone is looking out for their best interests, even if they have difficulty articulating it. Take the necessary steps before incapacitation may become an issue.
- Communicate well with siblings and loved ones. It is not uncommon for anxiety and fear to suddenly appear in anticipation of death.

CHAPTER 12

After Passing: Knowledge Becomes a Gift

There are many ways to honor the people we love when they are gone. When Margie passed, the grief was immediate, but it was notable that the chaos many families experience never came. Months earlier, her daughter Lisa had been helping as Financial Power of Attorney. Together they had organized Margie's accounts, documented where important papers were kept, and set aside funds for final expenses. When the executor, Margie's daughter Naomi, began settling the estate, Lisa was able to hand her a simple folder: passwords, account summaries, insurance contacts, estate attorney information, and the location of the will.

Instead of weeks of searching and guessing, the family spent their time remembering their mother. The legal authority of Financial Power of Attorney had ended the moment Margie passed but the clarity and preparation Lisa helped create became one final act of care for everyone she left behind

Legally, your role as the Financial Power of Attorney agent ends the moment your loved one passes, but the care, clarity, and insight you have provided up to this point become a pivotal gift.

Whether or not you are also named as the representative of the estate (Executor/Executrix), your familiarity with their financial life can be a great help during this transition. If someone else is stepping into the executor role, your knowledge of where documents are kept, how bills were paid, and what financial obligations exist can ease their burden and help ensure nothing is overlooked.

Your Helpful Role (unofficial, but crucial if needed)

- o   Share location of key documents
- o   Assist with death certificate procurement
- o   Help notify institutions: SSA, insurance companies, banks.
- o   Support the executor in closing accounts, distributing assets, and filing final taxes.

Golden Agreement Best Practices

- Your legal role as FPOA agent ends at death, but your insights become invaluable.
- Your familiarity with their financial life greatly helps the executor. If you are that person also, your advanced planning will be rewarded with time, money and stress savings.
- Your support helps prevent important transition items from being overlooked and carries forward their life story with respect.

Final Notes and Encouragement

We avoid hard conversations about aging because they force us to acknowledge a shift in the natural order that we are powerless to stop, and we stay silent out of a deep-seated resistance to a progression that will eventually take away the version of our parents, loved ones, and ourselves that we've always known. You may feel like you are figuring it out as you go, and that is very common. This role is not just about laws, documents and ledgers. It is about legacy. You cannot be expected to act with perfection, just love and compassion. Rely on your judgment, character, and ability to understand what matters most to your loved one. In moments of uncertainty, return to that.

Your role is to act with care, clarity, and integrity to honor their wishes and preserve their dignity. Trust you have what you need to help support the aging journey.

Glossary of Terms

Beneficiary Designations: A versatile estate planning tool that allows an owner to designate a specific person or entity to receive certain assets, such as life insurance policies or retirement plans, upon the owner's death. These assets generally transfer outside of the probate process.

Durable Power of Attorney (POA): A type of Power of Attorney that remains valid and effective even if the person granting the power (the principal) becomes disabled or incapacitated. A non-springing durable power of attorney becomes effective immediately upon its execution.

Estate Plan: The process by which an individual or family arranges the transfer of assets in anticipation of death, aiming to preserve wealth for intended beneficiaries and provide flexibility for the individual prior to death. It covers property transfer at death and other personal matters, and may or may not involve tax planning.

Executor: (Also called "personal representative" or "executrix") An individual or entity, typically named in a will, responsible for carrying out the provisions of the will and administering the deceased person's estate. This includes probating the will, collecting assets, paying debts and expenses, and distributing remaining assets to beneficiaries.

Fiduciary Duty: The highest standard of care recognized by law, requiring an individual (the fiduciary) to act for someone else's benefit while prioritizing that person's interests above their own. This includes demonstrating complete care, good faith, avoiding conflicts of interest, and maintaining accurate financial records.

Financial Power of Attorney (FPOA): A legal document that grants a designated individual (agent or attorney-in-fact) the authority to manage the financial affairs of the person who created the POA (the principal). This can include managing bank accounts, paying bills, handling investments, and conducting real estate transactions.

Intestacy Laws: State laws that determine who inherit a deceased person's assets when that person dies without a valid will (intestate). The estate of a person who has died intestate typically goes through probate court, and the state's intestacy rules determine the distribution of assets, usually to relatives.

Living Trust (Revocable Living Trust): A trust created during one's lifetime that can be revoked or amended at any time by the creator. It can provide a vehicle for managing property during life, authorize a trustee to manage property if the creator becomes incapacitated, and often allows assets transferred into it to avoid probate upon the creator's death.

Payable-on-Death (POD) / Transfer-on-Death (TOD) Accounts: Allow an account owner to designate a specific beneficiary who will receive the funds or assets in the account (such as bank accounts, investment accounts, or even real estate via a TOD deed) upon the owner's death, bypassing the probate process.

Power of Attorney (POA): A legal authorization that grants an agent or attorney-in-fact the authority to act on behalf of an individual (the principal). The authority granted can be broad or limited to specific matters, such as property, finances, investments, or medical care.

Principal (in POA): The person who grants the Power of Attorney (POA) to an agent, thereby giving that agent the authority to act on their behalf.

Probate: The formal legal process that validates a will, appoints an executor, oversees the administration of the deceased person's estate, and distributes assets to intended beneficiaries. Laws vary by state, and probate can be a time-consuming and costly process that may be avoided through certain estate planning tools.

Springing Power of Attorney (POA): A type of Power of Attorney that is executed immediately but does not become effective unless a specific triggering event occurs, such as the principal becoming incapacitated. This often requires certification by a medical professional.

Will: A legal document that outlines an individual's wishes for the distribution of their property after their death. To be legally valid, it typically requires the individual to be of legal age and mentally competent, to sign the document, and to have it witnessed by at least two adults.

*Source: American Bar Association

Golden Agreements: are thoughtful commitments that families and loved ones create together to support one another throughout the aging journey. Our mission is to help families prepare with clarity, compassion, and foresight—transforming what could become crisis management into intentional planning and deeper understanding.

At www.GoldenAgreements.com , you'll find resources and guidance to facilitate meaningful family conversations about aging, care, and support. We also offer free articles filled with practical ideas and insights to help you navigate these important discussions with confidence.

Aging In Place

Agencies versus Independent Aides

Difficult Conversations

Definitions and Terminology

Essentials in Medication Management

Making the Home Safe

and so much more.

Continue the Journey

If this guide helped you, the next step is implementation.

Visit www.GoldenAgreements.com to:

- o   Download structured worksheets
- o   See the selection of products curated by common aging challenges such as Fall Prevention, Medication Management, and Home Safety
- o   Access practical resources to support Financial Power of Attorney agents
- o   Facilitate meaningful family planning conversations

www.ingramcontent.com/pod-product-compliance
Lightning Source LLC
Chambersburg PA
CBHW032000140726
47988CB00019B/2906